AlphaBasiCs

The Computer
from A to Z

A Bobbie Kalman Book

Crabtree Publishing Company

AlphaBasiCs

Created by Bobbie Kalman

To Sophia and Thomas
Think big and shine bright!

Author and Editor-in-Chief
Bobbie Kalman

Managing editor
Lynda Hale

Project editor
Marsha Baddeley

Research and editing team
John Crossingham
Heather Levigne
Kate Calder

Computer design
Lynda Hale
John Crossingham
Campbell Creative Services (cover)

Production coordinator
Hannelore Sotzek

Separations and film
Dot 'n Line Image Inc.
CCS Princeton (cover)

Printer
Worzalla Publishing Company

Special thanks to
Ridley College—especially Diane Purdie, Danny Bang, Sean Porter, Vivek Rajakumar, Miguel Mori, Nikhil Joshi, Suchitra Joshi, Amira Archer-Davies, and Whitney Peterson; Peta-Gay Ramos; Nicola Hill; Sascha Hill; Blake Malcolm; David Pritchard; the students of John D. Parker School, Westview Secondary School, and Hoover Elementary School; Apple Computer, Inc.; Shannon Sliva and IBM Corporation; Netscape Communications Corporation; Simon Atkins and Dave Erskine, GeneratorIdeaWorks

Photographs
Apple Computer, Inc./Terry Hefferman: page 4 (top); Marc Crabtree: back cover, title page, pages 9, 16, 20, 21, 24, 25, 26, 30, 31; Christl Hill: page 22 (top); IBM Corporation: page 4 (bottom); Bobbie Kalman: pages 7 (bottom), 11, 22 (bottom), 29 (both); The Toronto Star/Ron Bull: cover, page 17; The Toronto Star/Rick Eglinton: page 19; other images by Digital Stock and Digital Vision; screen shots and icons reprinted with permission from Apple Computer, Inc. and Microsoft Corporation

Illustrations
Barbara Bedell: pages 5, 12-13, 14, 20
Bonna Rouse: page 15

Crabtree Publishing Company

350 Fifth Avenue	360 York Road, RR 4	73 Lime Walk
Suite 3308	Niagara-on-the-Lake	Headington
New York	Ontario, Canada	Oxford OX3 7AD
N.Y. 10118	L0S 1J0	United Kingdom

Cataloging in Publication Data

Kalman, Bobbie
The computer from A to Z

(AlphaBasiCs)
Includes index.

ISBN 0-86505-379-0 (library bound) ISBN 0-86505-409-6 (pbk.)
Computer words and concepts are discussed based on the alphabet.

1. Computers—Juvenile literature. [1. Computers. 2. Alphabet.]
I. Title. II. Series: Kalman, Bobbie. AlphaBasiCs.

QA76.23.K35 1999   j004   LC 98-41241
                                         CIP

Contents

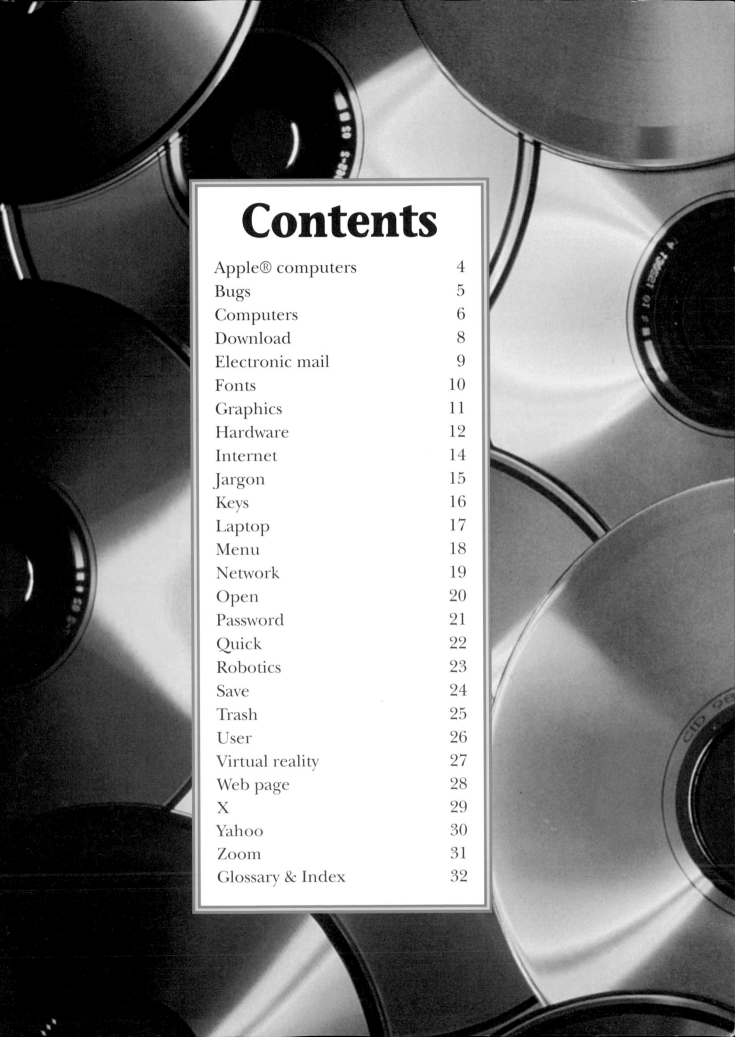

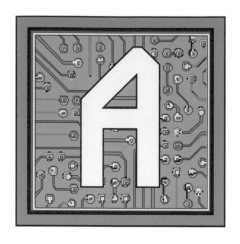

is for **Apple**® computers. An Apple®
computer is also known as a **Macintosh**®
or **Mac**®. Macs® were the first personal
computers that could be used to draw or
show pictures. **IBM**® is another type of
computer. Computers like IBMs® are
also called **personal computers**, or PCs.

Before Macintosh® *and IBM*®
*PCs were invented, computers were
so huge they took up entire rooms!
Now powerful computers can fit
right on your desk.*

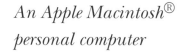

An Apple Macintosh®
personal computer

An IBM®
*personal
computer*

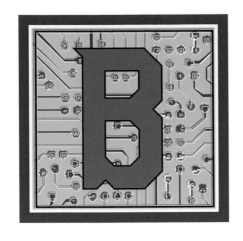

is for computer **bug**. This bug will not eat your computer, but it will bug you! A bug is a mistake in a computer program. It can cause problems with your printer or mouse, stop you from opening a program, or make it difficult to find your work.

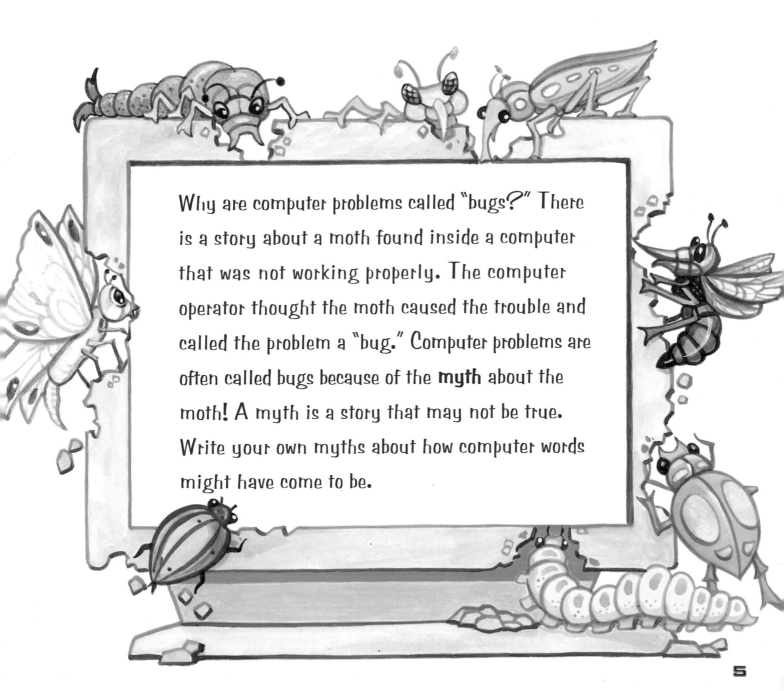

Why are computer problems called "bugs?" There is a story about a moth found inside a computer that was not working properly. The computer operator thought the moth caused the trouble and called the problem a "bug." Computer problems are often called bugs because of the **myth** about the moth! A myth is a story that may not be true. Write your own myths about how computer words might have come to be.

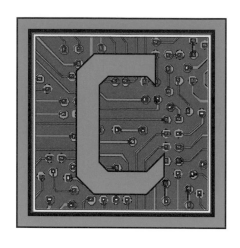

is for **computers**. You can use computers to find information, write stories, draw pictures, or play games. Computers are used in banks, hospitals, and schools. Cars and airplanes are built by machines that are run by computers. The space shuttle could not fly without them.

An ultrasonograph is a machine with a computer. It is used to look for problems inside a person's body.

Space shuttles are controlled by computers on the ground and in the shuttle.

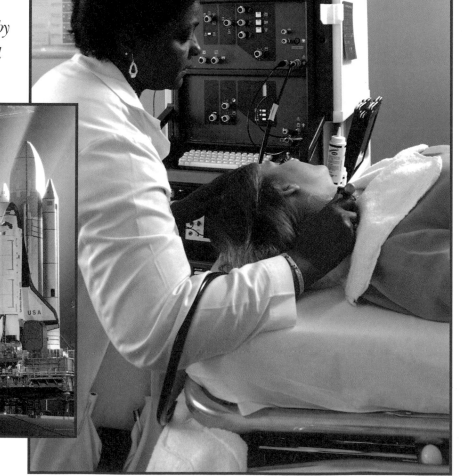

Factories use computers to make all kinds of products. This factory is making **solar panels**. Solar panels collect the energy of the sun.

Students use computers in schools for researching, writing, and solving math problems.

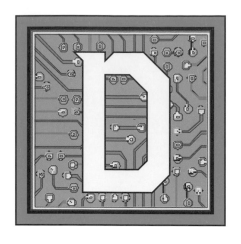

is for **download**. Taking files or programs from one computer and storing them on another computer is called downloading. Be careful when you download files. Sometimes a file may have a **virus**! A virus is a program that causes problems with your computer.

*You can download pictures, music, and computer games from the **Internet**. Some cost money. Free programs are called **freeware** or **shareware**. To learn more about the Internet, turn to the letter I on page **14**.*

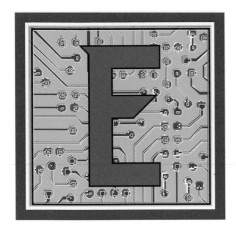

is for **electronic mail**, or **e-mail**. E-mail is a way of sending messages by computer. It is faster than regular mail—e-mail arrives in a few minutes! People use e-mail to send letters to family and friends who live next door or far away! You can also send pictures and music by e-mail.

E-mail users call regular mail "snail mail."

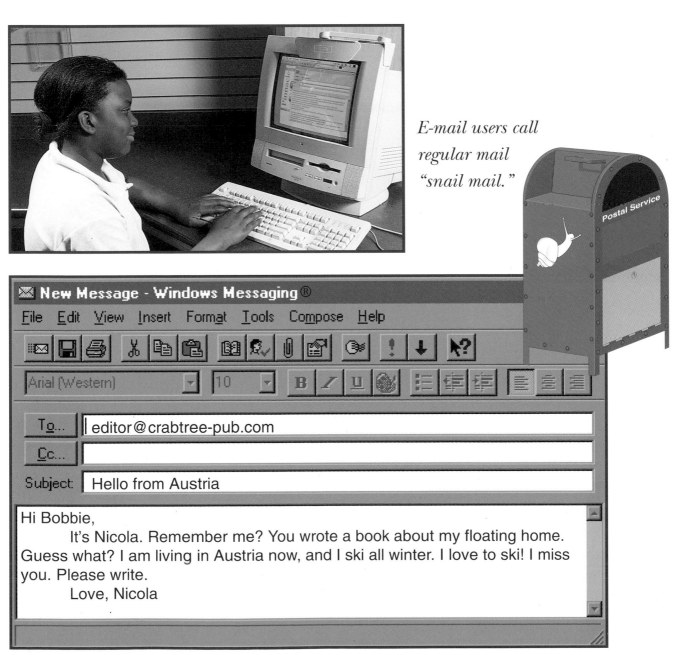

New Message - Windows Messaging®

File   Edit   View   Insert   Format   Tools   Compose   Help

Arial (Western)   10

To...   editor@crabtree-pub.com

Cc...

Subject: Hello from Austria

Hi Bobbie,
     It's Nicola. Remember me? You wrote a book about my floating home. Guess what? I am living in Austria now, and I ski all winter. I love to ski! I miss you. Please write.
     Love, Nicola

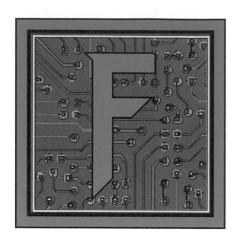

is for **font**. A font is the shape of a group of letters and numbers. You can change how a font looks by using **boldface** or *italic*. A font can be bigger or smaller, thinner or w i d e r. Look at the words in the blue box below. Each one is written in a different font.

Different fonts are used for different subjects! Look at the fonts in the box on the right. Which fonts would you use to write a:

letter to a friend

birthday card

newspaper

"KEEP OUT!"sign

KEEP OUT

school project

wedding invitation

Which font would you use to make your letter look handwritten by you?

Copacabana

Shaka Zulu

Goudy

Poetica Chancery

Lemonade

BUCKINGHAM

Times Roman

Sterling

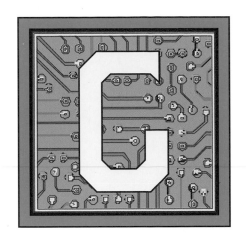

is for **graphics**. Graphics are pictures. You can draw pictures on a computer using a paint program. **Graphic artists** use pictures to make books look good. Do you have a publishing program at school? You can create a book and use graphics to make it more entertaining.

Nicola is designing a book using a desktop publishing program. She is putting her pictures and words together on the screen. She will then print out her book on a color printer.

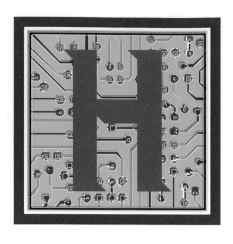

is for **hardware**. The computer parts you see on this page are called hardware. In order to operate a computer, you need a hard or floppy drive, a monitor, and a keyboard. What other types of hardware do the computers at your school have?

Speakers *make music and computer games sound better.*

A **monitor** *shows what you are doing on the computer.*

A **modem** *connects the computer to telephone lines or cables.*

A **mouse** *is used to point, click, and drag letters, words, or objects on the monitor.*

A mouse moves easily and stays clean on a **mouse pad**.

A **keyboard** *is used for typing letters, numbers, other characters, and commands.*

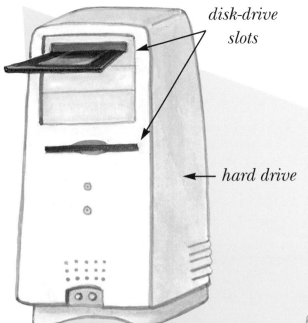

disk-drive slots

hard drive

A **scanner** is used to **scan**, or copy, pictures or information. After something is scanned, it can be viewed on the monitor and stored on disk as a file.

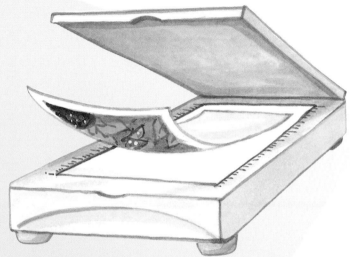

The **disk drive** is inside the computer. A disk drive reads and writes **data**, or information, on a disk. A floppy disk is placed into the disk drive through a thin slot. The **hard drive** is where the computer stores most data.

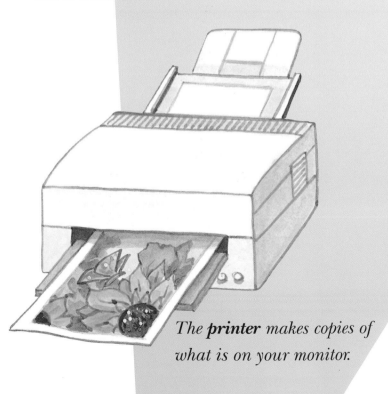

The **printer** makes copies of what is on your monitor.

Software are programs that tell the computer what to do. Each piece of hardware shown here needs software called **drivers** to help it work with the computer. Word processors, video games, and computer-art programs are examples of software. Software often comes on disks.

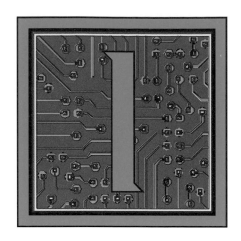

is for **Internet**. "Inter" means among. Net is short for **network**. Information is passed among a network of computers that are joined by wires, cables, or satellites. The Internet connects networks all over the world. You can use it to find information, download programs, or write to people.

WARNING!
When you are on the Internet, you must be very careful not to give anyone your name or address. If anything on the Internet makes you feel uncomfortable, tell an adult right away.

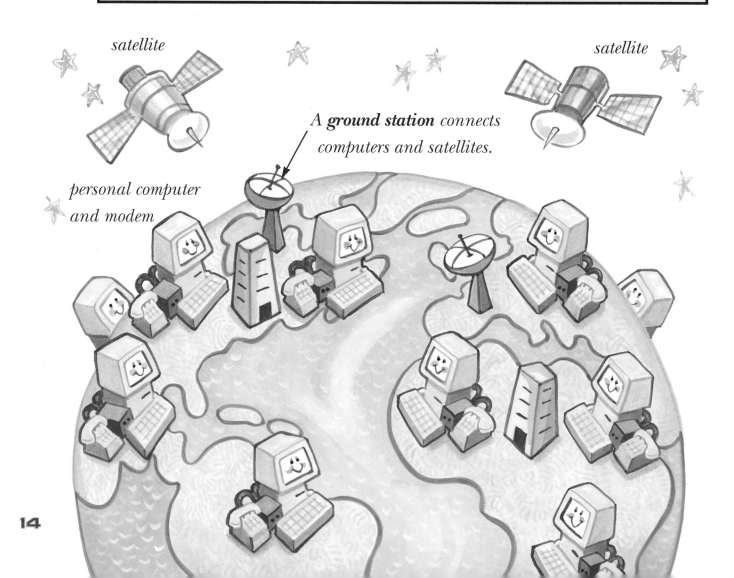

satellite

satellite

*A **ground station** connects computers and satellites.*

personal computer and modem

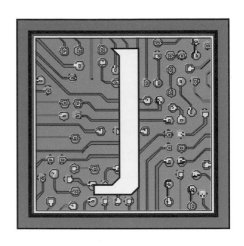

is for **jargon**. Jargon is language used to talk about a special subject. Nicknames and slang words are jargon. Computer jargon helps make difficult ideas easy to remember. "Surfing the net" is jargon that means "looking for information on the Internet."

1. bells and whistles

2. sneakernet

Match the jargon beside the pictures with the meanings below. Do not write in the book! Write down your answers on a piece of paper.

A. When a program failure causes the computer to **freeze**, or stop working
B. Extra features on computer hardware or programs, such as speakers and sound effects
C. A confusing computer program
D. Moving computer files by carrying a disk across the room to another computer
E. A place where information is lost
F. An old and useless computer

5. boat anchor

6. crash

4. bit bucket

3. spaghetti code

Answers

E:4, F:5
C:3, D:2,
A:6, B:1,

15

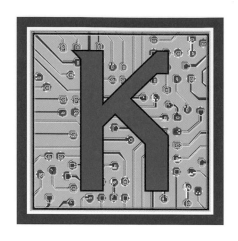

is for **keys**. Keys are the buttons on the keyboard. There are letter, number, symbol, and command keys. **Hotkeys** are two or more keys that are pressed at the same time. You can use hotkeys to stop printing, end a program, or restart your computer.

The computer keyboard is called a **QWERTY** keyboard because Q, W, E, R, T, and Y are its first six letters.

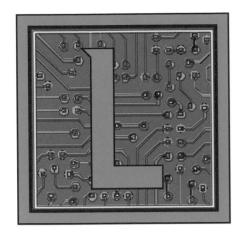

is for **laptop** computer. A laptop is a small computer that can be placed easily on your lap or on a table. The screen of the laptop folds down so the computer can be carried like a briefcase. Laptops are also called **notebook** computers because they are almost as small as a book.

In some schools, each student has a laptop for doing schoolwork. Laptops can be powered by electricity or battery.

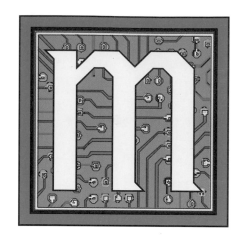

is for **menu**. A menu is a list of choices. A restaurant menu allows you to choose what you would like to eat. A computer menu lets you choose what you want to do on the computer. For example, if you want to leave a program, you can choose "exit" from the **File** menu.

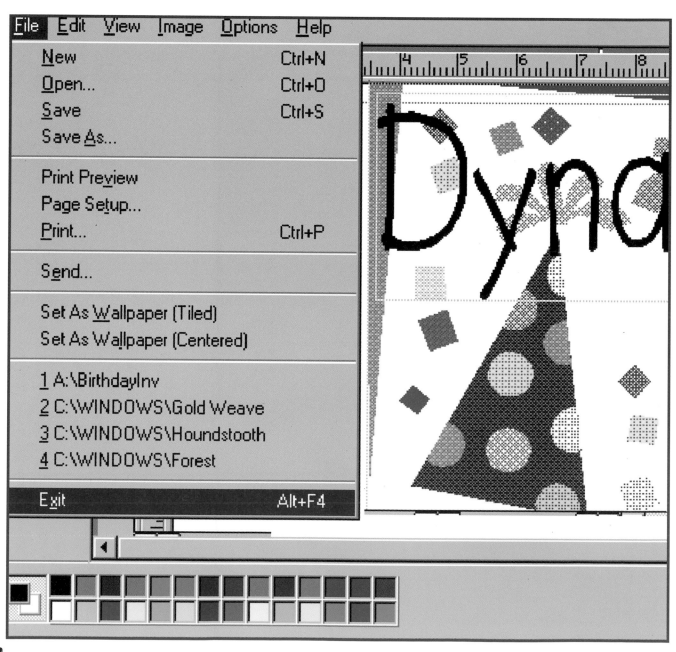

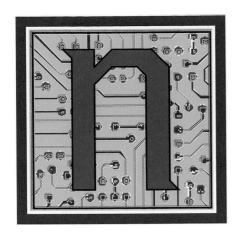 is for **network**. A network is a group of computers that are connected so they can share information. A network allows you to open a file that is on another computer. It also allows many computers to share hardware such as printers and scanners.

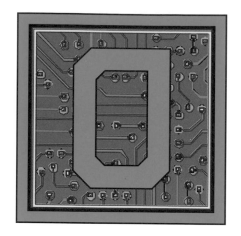

is for **open**. To see a computer file, you need to open it. You can open your homework files, games, e-mail, and many other programs. Double-clicking on a file with your mouse is the easiest way to open it. You can also go to your computer's menu and choose "open."

An octopus has a hard time opening a jar, but a click of a mouse will open a computer file.

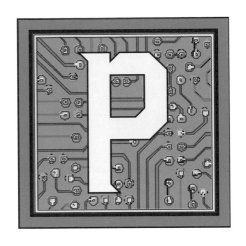

is for **password**. A password is a secret combination of letters or numbers that allows you to use the computer. Before you can start some programs, you need to type in your password. Programs need passwords when they contain information that only a few people are allowed to see.

A password should be words or numbers that are easy to remember but hard for others to guess. Your favorite color or middle name are not good passwords! Write down some good passwords and ask a friend to guess what they are.

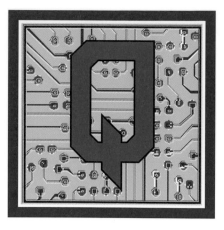

is for **quick**. Computers help you do things faster. You can scan a picture or correct the spelling in your homework quickly. Sometimes the speed of a computer can even help save lives! Computers warn people of storms, earthquakes, and other emergencies.

This boy is on a boat in the middle of the ocean. He is checking the computer for a weather report. If there is a storm coming, his family needs to know quickly!

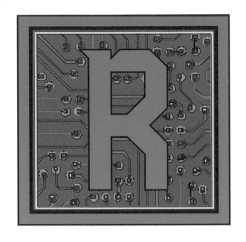

is for **robots**. Robots are machines that are run by computers. They are useful because they can lift heavy things and repeat motions quickly. Robots are used in factories and hospitals. They are also very important in police work because they can do difficult and dangerous jobs.

Thanks to this robot arm, astronauts may never have to leave the shuttle to fix this satellite!

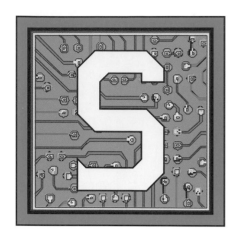

is for **save**. Your work is stored only while the computer is turned on, so you need to save it on a disk. A disk will store what you did even after it is taken from the drive. If you forget to save your work, it may be lost when the computer is turned off.

STOP

Always remember to **SAVE** *your work!*

Why do you think the boy in this picture is so upset?

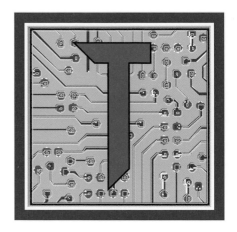

is for **trash**. There is an icon of a trash can on your screen. The trash can on your computer stores programs and files that you do not need anymore. To send files to the trash can, drag them to the trash-can icon. When you empty the trash, these files are deleted.

Icons are small pictures on a screen. If you click on these pictures with your mouse, you can make your computer perform tasks. Mac® computers use the Trash icon. Another type of trash icon is the **Recycle Bin**.

Trash

Recycle Bin

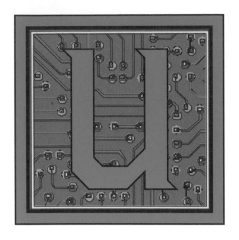

is for **user**. A user is a person who uses a computer. The first computers were difficult for most people to use. In order to make the computer work, users had to type in commands that were very difficult to remember. Today's computers are **user-friendly**, or easy to use.

Today's computers have replaced typed commands with icons. Icons sometimes look like the program you want to run, such as a paintbrush for a paint program. Now you do not have to remember a command to start your favorite program—just point and click!

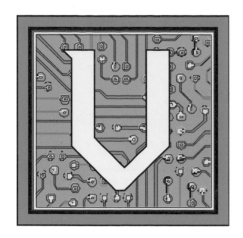

is for **virtual reality**. Virtual reality, or **VR**, is a type of computer program. VR combines graphics and sounds and, sometimes, equipment that moves. The user feels as if he or she is taking part in a real-life adventure. VR is even used to teach astronauts how to move in space.

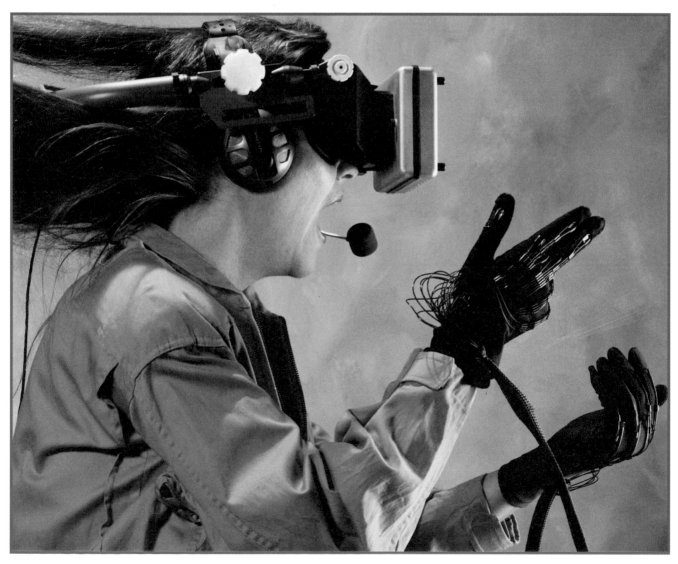

This woman is playing a VR program. The helmet she is wearing shows graphics and plays sounds. It also records the movements of her eyes. If she looks quickly to the left, the computer system will change the picture so she will feel as if she is actually turning a corner.

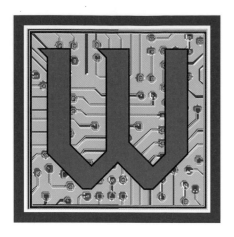

W is for **web page**. A web page is an Internet site that provides information. You can even take a tour of a museum on a web page. Many web pages are **linked**, or connected, on the **World Wide Web**. Find a web page that contains facts you can use for a school project.

Every web page has an address or **URL**. *URL stands for Universal Resource Locator. To see a web page, type its URL in the location box, shown above, and press enter.*

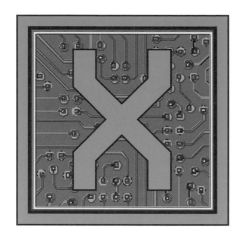

is for the letter **x** on the keyboard. The letter x is used as a shortcut to **cut** out words or pictures. It is like a pair of scissors. On a Macintosh® keyboard, hold down the **apple**®, or **command**, key and press x. On a PC keyboard, hold down the **control (ctrl)** key and press x.

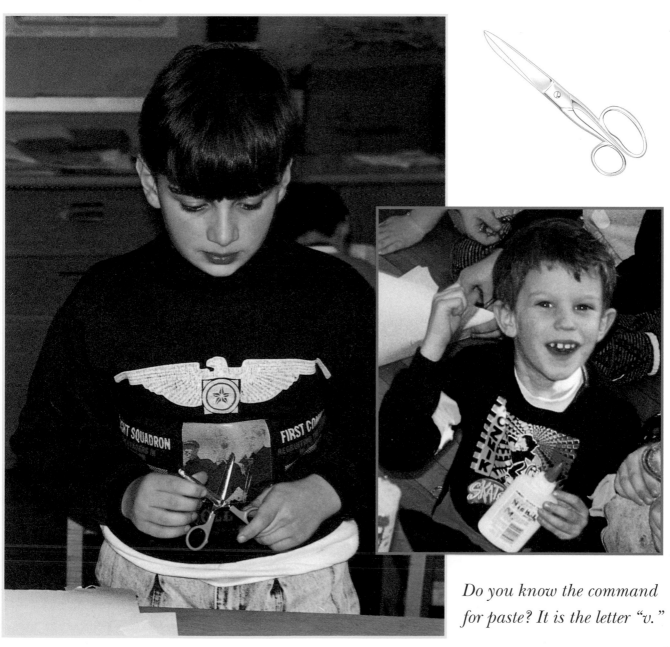

Do you know the command for paste? It is the letter "v."

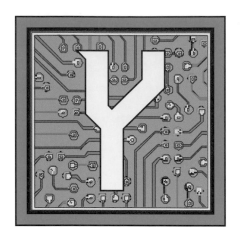

is for **Yahoo**! Yahoo is the name of a **search engine**. A search engine is a program used to search through large amounts of information on the World Wide Web. The address for Yahoo is www.yahoo.com. Y is also for, "Yahoo! I know how to use a computer!"

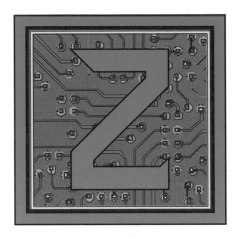

is for **zoom**. When pictures or words on the screen are either too small or big to see clearly, you can use zoom to change their size. Zooming in makes the picture appear bigger. Zooming out makes it appear smaller. You can see Whitney's smile better when you zoom in on her face!

The magnifying glass in your tool box helps you zoom in and out.

Words to know

bug A mistake in a computer program that causes problems with your computer

freeware Free software; also called shareware

ground station A system on Earth that connects satellites to computers by sending and receiving signals

hotkeys A combination of keys that perform a command when pressed at the same time

icons Small pictures that represent a program. Double-clicking on an icon will open a program.

link (n) An Internet address that connects to another Web site; (v) to connect

network A group of computers that shares hardware and software

PC A personal computer; usually refers to an IBM®-type computer

program A set of instructions that a computer carries out

satellite An object that travels around a planet in space to direct information

search engine A program used to search through large amounts of information on the Internet

user-friendly A term that describes computer programs that are easy to use

virus A program that causes problems with your computer

World Wide Web A service on the Internet that organizes information

Index

1 2 3 4 5 6 7 8 9 0   Printed in the U.S.A.   7 6 5 4 3 2 1 0 9 8